Finance and Economics Discussion Series: Constituencies and Legislation: The Fight over the McFadden Act of 1927

United States Federal Reserve Board,
Rodney Ramcharan, Rajan G. Raghuram

Finance and Economics Discussion Series
Divisions of Research & Statistics and Monetary Affairs
Federal Reserve Board, Washington, D.C.

Constituencies and Legislation: The Fight over the McFadden Act of 1927

Rodney Ramcharan and Rajan G. Raghuram

2012-61

Constituencies and Legislation: The Fight over the McFadden Act of 1927[1]

Raghuram G. Rajan
Booth School, University of Chicago

Rodney Ramcharan
Federal Reserve Board

Abstract

The McFadden Act of 1927 was one of the most hotly contested pieces of legislation in U.S. banking history, and its influence was still felt over half a century later. The act was intended to force states to accord the same branching rights to national banks as they accorded to state banks. By uniting the interests of large state and national banks, it also had the potential to expand the number of states that allowed branching. Congressional votes for the act therefore could reflect the strength of various interests in the district for expanded banking competition. We find congressmen in districts in which landholdings were concentrated (suggesting a landed elite), and where the cost of bank credit was high and its availability limited (suggesting limited banking competition and high potential rents), were significantly more likely to oppose the act. The evidence suggests that while the law and the overall regulatory structure can shape the financial system far into the future, they themselves are likely to be shaped by well organized elites, even in countries with benign political institutions.

[1] Raghuram Rajan: rajan@chicagobooth.edu, Rodney Ramcharan: Rodney.Ramcharan@frb.gov. We thank Edward Scott Adler, Daron Acemoglu, Lee Alston, Charles Calomiris, Price Fishback, Oded Galor, Sebnem Kalemli-Ozcan, Gary Richardson, Howard Rosenthal, Eugene White and seminar participants at the IMF, and the NBER Development of the American Economy and Income Distribution and Macroeconomic Groups for useful comments. Rajan thanks the Stigler Center for the Study of the State and the Economy and the Initiative on Global Markets, both at the University of Chicago's Booth School, as well as the National Science Foundation, for funding. Keith T. Poole and Kris James Mitchener kindly provided data.

Constituencies or interest groups that arise from the pattern of land holdings or other forms of economic production in a country can shape important economic institutions such as the financial system, and consequently, economic development (Engerman and Sokoloff (2002, 2003), Haber (2005), Rajan and Ramcharan (2011)). But the channel through which interest groups might operate remains a matter of debate. Some (see, for example, Acemoglu, Johnson, and Robinson (2005)) argue that the mediating channel is political institutions, as elite interest groups create coercive political institutions that give them the power to hold back the development of economic institutions, such as finance, and hence economic growth. However, legislation, and its effects on perpetuating rents and hence political power, may be another principal channel through which constituencies might shape the financial system and project their influence through time, even in benign democratic political systems (see Do (2004), Glaeser, Scheinkman, and Shleifer (2004), or Mian et. al (2010), for example).

In this paper, we study whether, and how, constituencies influence the development of the financial system, using evidence from congressional voting on the McFadden Act of 1927. The United States has long had a dual banking system, where state banks are chartered and regulated at the state level, while national banks operate under federal oversight. Before the McFadden Act, some states allowed state banks to open multiple branches, while others prohibited all branching. However, nationally chartered banks were, in all cases, not allowed to open branches (Cartinhour and Westerfield (1980), Southworth (1928)). As a result, an increasing number of national banks gave up their charter (which typically meant their leaving the Federal Reserve

System also).[2] The McFadden Act attempted to level the playing field by forcing states to accord largely the same branching rights to national banks as to state banks (Preston (1927)). It was the key piece of federal legislation regulating bank branching, and hence bank competition, in the United States for about 70 years—up until the passage of the Riegle-Neal Act in 1994.

The act proved enormously controversial, and a study of how the vote of each congressional district varied with the constituencies in that district can be extremely informative on (1) whether constituencies had political influence; and (2) whether the influence was directed in expected ways for, or against, greater competition and financial development. Of course, there has already been an enormous amount of work on the political economy of the McFadden Act (see, for example, Economides, Hubbard, and Palia (1996)). Much of the work has examined whether legislators from states with unit banks voted disproportionately against the Act, and the results are mixed at best – for instance, Economides, Hubbard, and Palia (1996) find that the influence of the proportion of banks with branches in the state on the fraction of state representatives voting for branching is negative and insignificant (though they find that states with poorly capitalized state banks voted against branching). Our contribution is to dive deeper into the determinants of the constituencies against branching within state. This allows us to focus on a richer, and more detailed, pattern of interests than previously examined, as

---

[2] The Comptroller of Currency in 1922 observed: "National banks are compelled to compete with state institutions. If state laws are more liberal they will constitute an inducement to banks to operate under the laws of the states rather than the Nation...If the system is to be perpetuated there must be national banks in sufficient number and strength...they must be given charters liberal enough to remain in the system. The advantage of the more liberal conditions that can be enjoyed outside the national banking system...will presently become a menace to the strength, and may ultimately threaten the very existence, of the Federal Reserve System (Report of the Comptroller of Currency (1922)).

well as exploit within state differences in voting patterns. Unlike previous work, we find strong evidence of constituency influence.

In Rajan and Ramcharan (2011), constituencies do appear to influence the structure of the financial sector. Specifically, landed elites—a key political constituency during this period--were successful in restricting local bank competition in different counties in the United States. Counties where the agricultural elite had disproportionately large land holdings had significantly fewer banks per capita, even correcting for state level effects. Moreover, credit appears to have been costlier, and access to it more limited, in these counties.

The literature suggests three main reasons why landed interests might have opposed more local bank competition. First, limits on bank competition and control over exit could provide landowners insurance during periods of agricultural distress. While large national banks or state banks with branches could foreclose more easily on loans and exit the locality, transferring capital to urban or less distressed rural areas, small local banks would have fewer options, and would have to continue lending to large local farmers during periods of distress (Calomiris and Ramirez (2004)).

Second, control over bank entry could accord landed interests greater influence over the local financial system, enabling them to prevent or delay the emergence of alternative centers of economic power and status (Chapman (1934)). For example, a rapidly growing manufacturing sector could increase the returns to schooling and attract labor away from agriculture, and there is evidence that landed interests may have used their political influence to restrict not just finance, but education and other public goods (Galor et. al (2009), Ramcharan (2010)).[3]

Third, large landowners generated surpluses which they could lend. They also often had a stake in, or influence over, the local bank. The entry of more formal credit institutions could be competition for their lending business. They also had indirect reasons to keep out competition in lending. Landowners often owned the local store. Tenants and small farmers needed credit to buy supplies from the local store. By limiting credit from alternative sources – for instance by keeping banks out -- the local merchant cum landlord could lock the farmer in and charge exorbitant prices, perpetuating the lucrative debt peonage system (Haney (1914, p55-56).[4][5] There is, however, some controversy among economic historians about the extent of debt peonage and the "bankability" of tenant farmers and share croppers during this period.[6]

---

[3] Alston and Ferrie (1993) argue that because landed interests wanted to maintain a paternalistic state in order to ensure a steady supply of farm labor, the Southern congressional delegation systematically blocked the development of the federal welfare state in the U.S. until mechanization reduced the demand for unskilled labor.

[4] Initially, there was a conflict of interest between large landlords and the local merchant because both had an interest in tenant farmers. But "as time went on the two classes tended more and more to become one." Landlords were drawn into the store business by "the desirability of supplying their tenants ", while "storekeepers frequently became landowners by taking over the farms of those who were indebted to them or by direct purchase at the prevailing low price". Hicks (1931, p32). Haney (1914, p54) writes that in most parts of central Texas, "over 90 percent of those tenants who owe the store are also indebted to their landlords for larger or smaller advances." See also the surveys in Goodwyn (1978) and Ransom and Sutch (2001).

[5] There were other benefits for the rich landlord to limiting access. Landlords would also enjoy a competitive advantage, for instance by being able to buy land cheaply when small farmers were hit by adversity, or by having privileged access to loans in the midst of a prolonged drought.

[6] For example, the evidence in Fishback (1989) suggests that most farmers may have been able to repay their debts shortly after harvests. Also, while debt peonage is most closely associated with racial discrimination, Alston and Kauffman (2001) find little evidence of discrimination in sharecropper pay for a sample of southern counties. However, the most extreme versions of debt peonage (forced land sales because of distress, racial discrimination, etc.) need not apply for landowners cum storeowners to have an incentive to monopolize credit.

5

While we know the landed elite had the incentive and the ability to influence outcomes, we do not know whether their influence worked through the political process. For instance, Rajan and Ramcharan (2011) argue that landed elites could have shaped local bank competition by giving business to favored banks. Indeed, if politicians were strictly motivated by doing good for the mass of voters (the public interest view of legislation), it seems unlikely that they would have sided with the views of the landed interests. If, however, concentrated money power trumped dispersed voter interests, one might expect a district's politicians to reflect the interests of the landed elite (the private interest view).[7] If so, we should see representatives of districts where landed elites were important vote disproportionately against the McFadden Act.

The McFadden Act proposed to extend bank branching powers to national banks only in those states that already allowed state banks the right to open branches. Contemporary texts (see, for example, Preston (1927)) suggest that the expectation was that if the McFadden Act allowed national banks liberal branching powers, then subsequent to the passage of the act, national banks would unite with large state banks to push for branching in all states. Thus landed elites in non-branching states could be expected to be even more opposed to the McFadden Act than were landed elites in branching states, especially because the latter's rents would already have been diminished by branching by state banks.

---

[7] There is evidence that local politicians had some influence over bank structure, over and above their votes on legislation. For example, members of Congress often influenced bank chartering decisions in their district. Referring to state charter applications, American Bankers Association (1935) quotes a Comptroller on political influence: "prior to the disposition of an application a copy thereof is sent to the national-bank examiner, to the *Member of Congress for the district in which the bank is located,* and to the superintendent of the state banking department, with request for information on the character and standing of the applicants, the existing demand for a bank at the locality, and an expression of opinion as to whether success is probable."

The Act evolved in Congress as constituencies worked to influence the legislation. Examining the initial congressional roll call data, controlling for state fixed effects (which allow us to absorb state differences in regulations, among other factors), we find that congressmen from districts with more concentrated land holdings (our proxy for the relative importance of landed interests) were far more likely to oppose the McFadden Act during its first House vote in 1926. The results are stronger still when we instrument land concentration with a technological determinant of the optimal size of land holdings, the pattern of rainfall in the area.

The association of land concentration with congressional opposition was especially strong in those districts where agriculture was relatively more important than manufacturing, suggesting that landed elites were politically more effective when they also dominated economically. Similarly, the association of landed interests with congressional opposition was particularly strong in non-branching states, perhaps because of the fears of the local elite about the incipient spread of branching.

Also, using hand collected data from the 1930 Census on measures of credit cost and access, such as the interest rate and loan to value ratios of farms, we find that congressional support for the McFadden Act, was significantly lower in those districts with high credit costs and limited credit availability, suggesting that the desire to protect incumbents' rents may have indeed inspired political opposition to the Act.

We use the legislative history of the McFadden Act to help identify more precisely the role of landed interests in shaping its passage. Some of the more aggrieved landowners, especially those in smaller communities, were appeased by provisions that were introduced into the act limiting the ability of national banks to open branches in small towns. The historical commentary also suggests that political horse-trading in the House may have been key in securing the Act's final passage, as government price support for grain was extended to cotton and tobacco, allegedly in order to entice the Southern delegation to support the McFadden Bill and break the deadlock with the Senate (the House disagreed with the Senate version that was more favorable towards bank competition). Consistent with this narrative, we find evidence that the association between congressional opposition and the strength of landed elites declined significantly in tobacco growing districts, ensuring the Act's passage.

Finally, using county level data, we explore the impact of the Act on local banking structures. There is evidence that in those states allowing branching, the Act's passage did lead to faster national bank growth, and a decline in deposits held in state banks. The legislation thus had a significant impact on local bank structures.

Eventually, technological changes in banking, which allowed banking at a distance, made it hard to maintain bank branching restrictions in the US (Kroszner and Strahan (1999)). The Riegle-Neal Act repealed the remaining restrictions on bank branching in 1994. A summary evaluation then is that by restricting the scope of the McFadden Act and protecting small banks from competition, landed interests strengthened small community banks, which gained political influence and maintained the protections long after their initial protectors lost their economic and political heft. Thus constituencies can have influence long after they pass from the scene.

Ours is not the first paper to show that landed interests matter for financial development (see, for example, Rajan and Ramcharan (2011), and Vollrath (2009)). While Rajan and Ramcharan (2011) argue that landed interests have influence that helps them restrict local bank entry and competition, they do not provide evidence of such influence working through political channels and congressional votes. The pattern of voting on the McFadden Act helps us establish the necessary link between landed interests and political influence.

Finally, there is an extensive literature on the political economy of banking legislation more generally (for recent examples, see Acharya, van Nieuwerburgh, Richardson and White (2011), Brown and Dinc (2005), Dinc (2005), Cetorelli and Strahan (2006), Mian, Sufi, and Trebbi (2010), or Igan, Mishra, and Tressel (2011)). Our incremental contribution to the widely accepted finding that narrow directly-affected interest groups influence legislation is to demonstrate the influence of deeper (possibly technologically-determined) constituencies that drove one of the most salient pieces of financial legislation in U.S. history.

In the next section we briefly describe the Act. We describe the data in section III, the main results are in section IV, we discuss the impact of the act on bank structures in section V, and then conclude.

I. THE MCFADDEN ACT

The Federal Reserve Act of 1913 did not grant national banks branching rights. National bank regulators therefore feared that the national banks would not be competitive with state banks in states that allowed state banks branching powers. The Comptroller of the Currency ruled in 1922 that national banks could open intra-city offices for the purpose of collecting deposits when this did not conflict with state laws (see White (1985)). Two days after the Comptroller's ruling, the First National Bank of St. Louis opened a full-fledged branch and argued that, as a federally chartered institution, it was not subject to state regulation. Two years later, the Supreme Court ruled against it, but the fight had been joined.

Fearing that once the national banks got branching powers, they would join large state banks in pressing for branch banking in every state, banks in many of the unit banking states formed state associations that declared themselves opposed to branch banking. On the national level, the United States Bankers Association Opposed to Branch Banking was formed. Unit bankers pressed their state legislatures to remove any ambiguity about whether branching banking was prohibited, and by 1924, nine states added anti-branching provisions to their banking laws.

The McFadden Act was motivated by the federal government's desire to resolve the ambiguity about the powers of national banks, and preserve the attractiveness of national bank charters and membership in the nascent Federal Reserve System against regulatory competition from state bank regulators. It provided that in states where state branch banking existed, or could exist in the future, both national and state bank members of the Federal Reserve System would be allowed to operate branches within the city limits of the parent bank. This was viewed as a step towards further branching liberalization and greater bank competition at the local level.

The local political constituencies who had historically guarded their control of the banking system saw their rents threatened by the prospect of increased competition and the potential dominance of local banking by large national banks. Moreover, as discussed above, they feared that the Act would lead to more states opening up to branching. Opposition to branching was also intense in those areas with many small unit banks. The 1920s was a period of agricultural distress, and rural small bank failures became increasingly common. These unit bankers feared that the introduction of bank branching

and the entry of large national banks into small towns could accelerate small bank

failures. The Mid West, especially Chicago, heavily populated with small unit banks,

became the epicenter of opposition to the McFadden Act (see Chapman and Westerfield

(1980), Southworth (1928), White (1985)).

As an aside, we should note that while the landed elite may have been concerned

by the pro-competitive aspects of the McFadden Act, Populist forces may have pushed

for preserving unit banking because it limited the power of distant bankers. Politics

makes strange bedfellows -- different constituencies may make common cause over

regulations because they like different aspects of it, even though the constituencies

fundamentally oppose each other. Moreover, popular populist policies – keep banking

local – may capture the public's imagination even if they are not broadly good for the

populace, or framed with their interests in mind. Our detailed examination of district-by-

district voting patterns can help us focus on local influences, which may be lost if we

were to examine state-level voting patterns, as some previous studies have done.

The Act went through several metamorphoses in Congress, as the various

constituencies sought to influence the legislation. In its original form, before February of

1926, the branching issue was phrased in language widely viewed as favoring further

branching and local competition.[8] But the Hull amendment, which delayed the Act's

passage amid much controversy, sought to "limit bank branching to those States which

permitted branch banking *at the time of the approval of the bill*—so far as the national

---

[8] Specifically, this version of the Act "provided that state bank members of the Federal Reserve System
might not establish branches outside their home cities and that national banks might establish branches in
their home cities in those states where state banks were accorded a like privilege "Collins, "Report on the
Bank Branching Question", pp 82-83.

banking and the Federal Reserve Systems are concerned." In so doing, the amendment was intended to preserve the coalition against the spread of branching, thus allowing the act to obtain support from unit-banking states. That is, the Hull amendment would ensure that any subsequent legislation to permit branching would encounter three-fold opposition from (1) national banks that could not now have branches in those states (2) the state bank members of the Federal Reserve System, who also could not have any branches in those states (3) and of course, the incumbent unit bankers. The Hull amendment was dropped from the final bill before it passed.

In sum, the sections pertaining to branching in the Act were vigorously contested, right from the Act's introduction in the House in 1922 through its final passage in 1927, which was assured only after the Senate invoked a cloture motion for the third time in its history at that point. The Act was signed into law by President Coolidge in February 1927.

Clearly, unit banks were opposed to the Act. But what interests lay behind the unit banks? As we argue in the introduction and in Rajan and Ramcharan (2011), landed agrarian interests were strongly opposed to any reforms perceived to be fostering more local bank competition. In what follows, we will attempt to tease out the role of these deeper interests in opposing competition.

II. Data

A. Land Concentration

What could be a proxy for the strength of landed interests and their desire to limit access to finance? In any of these hypotheses where there is a group of larger farmers who "exploit", there has to be another group of small farmers or tenants who are explicitly "exploited" (as in the debt peonage hypothesis) or are implicitly "exploited" (for instance, if they contribute savings to the local pool but do not get loans in a downturn because their access to finance is deliberately left underdeveloped, as in Calomiris and Ramirez (2004)). One measure of the strength of these two constituencies is the Gini coefficient of land farmed, which measures the degree of inequality of land holdings. If land holdings are very unequal, large landowners could have both the ability and incentive to limit access to finance, while if land holdings are relatively equal (whether uniformly large or small), no one has the power or the interest to alter access for others.[9]

Our measure of the concentration of land holdings is based on the distribution of farm sizes as in Rajan and Ramcharan (2011). The data are collected by the U.S. Census Bureau at the county level for 1920. A farm is defined as "all the land which is farmed by one person, either by his own labor alone or with the assistance of members of his household or hired hands". Note that a tenant is also a farmer by this definition. We have information on the number of farms falling within particular acreage categories or bins, ranging from below 3 acres up to 1000 acres. Assuming the midpoint of each bin is the average size of farms in that bin, we construct the Gini coefficient to summarize the farm acreage data (see Appendix for a precise formula and definitions). The Gini coefficient is a measure of concentration that lies between 0 and 1, and higher values indicate that farms at both ends of the size distribution account for a greater proportion of total agricultural land—that is, the holding of agricultural land is unequally distributed.

---

[9] This presupposes, of course, that those without land either do not have the basic minimum surplus to be worth squeezing (such as field hands) or live in towns, far from the sphere of influence of the landlords. We will show that a greater fraction of activity in manufacturing (a measure of non-land activity) does diminish the effect of land concentration on opposition to the Act.

In 1920, the average Gini coefficient of a county is 0.426, the 99th percentile county is at 0.687, the 1st percentile county is at 0.2, and the standard deviation is 0.10. The correlation between the Gini for a county and the share of agricultural land in small farms (below 20 acres) is positive, as is the correlation with the share in large farms (above 175 acres). The correlation between the Gini and the share in medium sized farms (between 20 acres and 175 acres) is negative. Thus counties with high Gini coefficients tend, as we would expect, to have more land in both small, as well as large, farms. Interestingly, as a result of the greater weight in small farms, counties with Gini above median have smaller farms on average than counties with Gini below median.

This pattern of correlations between the Gini coefficient and farm sizes suggest that agricultural production might have been increasingly dominated by a landed elite in those counties with a higher Gini coefficient. Figure 1 indicates that the Southern and Border counties, areas known for plantation agriculture, generally had higher Gini coefficients than elsewhere. Similarly, the correlations in Table 2 suggest that areas with high levels of land concentration tended to have higher levels of rainfall, a key requirement for plantation crops like cotton and sugar; counties with higher Gini coefficients also tended to specialize less in grain and other crops more suited to independent smaller family farms, given the technologies of the era (see Ramcharan (2010) and the references contained therein). All this also suggests that land concentration was determined substantially by technological forces outside finance.

B. Congressional District Votes

The McFadden Act was first introduced into the 69th Congress on Feb 4th, 1926. There is a weak positive correlation between the percent of a state's congressional delegation that voted against the Act and the average level of land concentration within that state in 1920. But the voting behavior of House members, in contrast to the Senate, is designed to reflect the interests of local constituents rather than aggregate state level issues, and we focus more systematically on the district level voting data (see Rusk (2001) and references contained therein).

To this end, we merge the detailed county level data on land concentration and other demographic, geographic, and economic variables with the congressional district voting data on the McFadden Act. There are about 3000 counties surveyed in 1920 Census, but only 427 districts in the 69th Congress, which were apportioned based on the population estimates from the 1920 Census. In about 330 cases there is a direct correspondence between congressional districts and counties: one or more whole counties are aggregated into a single district. In these cases, we construct the district level data by aggregating the "whole" county level data using basic measures of central tendency such as the mean and weighted by each county's relative size in the district. For instance, the First congressional district of Maine is comprised of both Cumberland and York counties, and we use the population weighting scheme: each county's characteristic is attributed to the First district in proportion to the county's relative population in the district.

However, for about 20 districts, counties have either been split into several districts, or pieces of various counties and towns have been combined to form a district. We call these cases "splits" and they primarily occur in urban areas. For example, Manhattan (New York county) was "split" or divided into 11 different districts in the 69th Congress. For county level data in the "split" districts, we simply ascribe the county's characteristics uniformly to those districts contained within the county (Adler

(2002)). Some districts were however formed from towns and were omitted from the sample as there is no correspondence with county level data. We are thus left with a sample of 354 congressional districts.

In Table 3A, we decompose the initial vote on Feb 4th, 1926, and this suggests that the voting pattern in the available sample of districts is similar to the full roll call data – 66 percent voted Yea and 23 percent voted Nay in the available sample versus 67 percent and 21 percent respectively in the full roll call vote. And while 80 percent of House Republicans and only 47 percent of the Democrats voted in favor of the act, this difference in support across party lines largely reflected varying regional economic interests rather than ideological differences (Southworth (1928)). For instance, from Table 3B we see that opposition was mainly concentrated in the agrarian South, and parts of the upper mid West.

The correlation between land concentration and a "Nay" vote is 0.17, which is significant at the 5 percent level. Also, Figure 2, which plots the distribution of land concentration by "Yea" and "Nay" votes, suggests that House members from districts with a greater similarity in the size of land holdings—"more equal counties"—were far more likely to vote in favor of the legislation than those from more unequal districts. These differences across the two distributions are significant at the one percent level. Of course, this non parametric evidence is only suggestive; omitted demographic, geographic, and economic variables might explain the motivation for opposition to the Act, rather than simply the influence of landed interests. We thus use the legislative history of the Act to understand the role of landed interests in shaping the legislation.

III. RESULTS: LAND CONCENTRATION AND THE MCFADDEN ACT

A. THE INITIAL BILL, 1926

To this end, in the first two columns in Table 4A we use a simple linear probability model to measure the relationship between land concentration within a congressional district and the probability that the district's representative voted against the McFadden Act in its initial form on February 4th 1926. Specifically, omitting the abstentions and paired votes, the dependent variable equals 1 if a congressman voted against the act, and 0 if he voted "Yea". We also include state-level indicator variables in all specifications to control for the potential impact of state level factors on the House vote. These correct for state level differences in regulations such as unit versus branch banking and presence of deposit insurance, as well as other differences such as average capital levels (Economides, Hubbard, and Palia (1996)) that the prior literature has focused on.[10]

Consistent with the non-parametric evidence, there is a statistically significant and large positive relationship between the probability of a "Nay" vote and land concentration in column 1. A one standard deviation increase in land concentration is associated with a 0.05 increase in the probability of observing a "Nay" vote; recall that the unconditional probability of a "Nay" vote in the sample is 0.26.

There are, of course, important district-level differences we should correct for. We include a broad array of geographic and demographic controls in Table 4A column 2.

---

[10] The bicameral nature of the Congress and the design of House terms are intended to make House members more responsive to local interests than the Senate, but aggregate state and regional factors might still affect House voting patterns. For example, state level "machine" politics might sway the House delegation from a given state to vote in a particular way. Likewise, broad regional interests—the Mid West and South were far more agrarian than other parts of the country—could also sway the voting behavior of a state's House delegation (Rusk (2001)).

Waterways were centers of economic activity as well as transportation (and if freshwater, of irrigation). For instance, waterways such as the Great Lakes in the upper mid west, and the Atlantic Ocean along the East coast helped spur industrialization and the demand for financial services in those regions (Pred (1966)). And including these variables help control for plausibly exogenous determinants of a district's prosperity and the kind of economic activity it might undertake. The socioeconomic controls include: the fraction of the district's population that is illiterate, the fraction that is young, and the fraction that is black. Also included are the log of district population, as well as the fraction of the population that is urban (reflecting the fact that urban interests vis a viz banking might have differed from rural groups).

In addition, we also include as controls the ideology index developed by Poole and Rosenthal (2007) for each congressman voting on the Act. The first dimension of the index is generally interpreted as the congressman's preference for redistribution—liberal or conservative bias. The second dimension focuses on urban relative to agrarian biases. Since both dimensions probably influenced voting on the act, we include both indices, recognizing that we may be overcorrecting since the landed elite might well determine the ideological preferences of the congressman in power. In this, our baseline specification, the coefficient estimate on land concentration in Table 4 column 2 nearly doubles, and remains significant at the 5 percent level.

The concentration of land holdings might be related to the value of land ownership itself, and there is some evidence that the value of landownership may have directly affected preferences for different types of bank structures. For example, Calomiris and Ramirez (2004) find evidence that unit banking was more likely in states with higher farm wealth, suggesting that the returns to preserving local bank lending might have been higher in those states where land was more valuable. In column 3, we control for the per capita farm wealth within the congressional district—the value of land, crops, buildings and implements divided by the farm population. The coefficient estimate on land concentration increases slightly in magnitude, suggesting it is not a proxy for per-capita farm wealth. Interestingly, per capital farm wealth, while positive, is not statistically significant. Also, because the land concentration measure does not distinguish between forms of ownership, in results available upon request, we control for the share of tenant farmers within the congressional district. This variable is not significant (p-value=0.63), while the land concentration coefficient is largely unchanged relative to column 2.

Land concentration may not be exogenous to banking structure. For instance, areas with small, and relatively few, banks may have relatively concentrated banking markets, which in turn may result in land concentration. Put differently, our discussion above has been based on an assumption that land concentration is the deeper driving variable. To address concerns about this assumption (and to place identification on firmer ground), we exploit the variation in land concentration that can arise from the plausibly exogenous variation in rainfall.

Rainfall patterns can shape the pattern of agricultural production. Plantation crops, such as cotton and sugar, are better suited to areas with plentiful rainfall, while wheat and grain, which were often grown on smaller more uniform plot sizes during this period, thrive in areas with less precipitation (Gardner (2002), Tomich, Kilby and Johnston (1995) and the references in Rajan and Ramcharan (2011)). Consistent with these ideas, there is a large first stage conditional correlation between land concentration and the log average rainfall in the district—reported in the notes to Table 4A.

In column 4, we use average rainfall as an instrument for land concentration. The IV results are less precisely estimated (p-value=0.09), but the coefficient is about 80 percent larger than the OLS estimate in column 2. As a robustness check, in column 5, we include both the average rainfall, as well as its standard deviation jointly as instruments. The latter is a common measure of weather risk, and has also been shown to affect the pattern of land holdings in the United States during this period (Ramcharan (2010)). As described in the notes to Table 4A, both variables are individually and jointly positively associated with land concentration. The estimates for instrumented land concentration in columns 4 and 5 are similar, and the over-identification test that the availability of two instruments permits us lends some plausibility to the exclusion restriction assumption, suggesting that land concentration in the district may have played an economically important role in shaping voting outcomes.

While the results using the rainfall instrument are reassuring about the direction of causality, congressional districts club together areas with varied rainfall patterns. This introduces noise, which is especially problematic when we split the sample, as some robustness tests require. Therefore, in the robustness exercises that follow, we will revert to the more conservative OLS estimates, though IV estimates are available on request.

In Table 4B, we perturb the baseline specification in a number of different ways in order to better understand the role of landed interests on voting outcomes. The relative economic clout of agrarian interests within a district might affect their ability to influence the political process. During this period the manufacturing sector, an important consumer of financial services, was growing, and becoming increasingly politically powerful. And in those districts where the economic power of the agricultural sector was offset by the power of the manufacturing sector, the influence of land concentration on congressional voting behavior might have been more muted. Conversely, in districts in which landed interests were the dominant economic power, they would likely wield greater political power, and thus, have greater influence over congressional district voting behavior.

We thus exploit the variation in the underlying economic structure across districts in order to understand better the possible role of landed interests and other constituencies in shaping the legislation. One measure of the relative economic power of the manufacturing sector is the ratio of the value of manufacturing output to the value of manufacturing and agriculture output in 1920. In Table 4B Column 1, we include the interaction between manufacturing share and land concentration in our baseline regression, taking care to include manufacturing share and its square directly. The estimates suggest that the positive impact of land concentration on congressional opposition to the Act was significantly more muted in those districts in which manufacturing was economically more important. For a district at the 25 percentile share of manufacturing in output, a one standard deviation increases in land concentration is associated with a 0.18 increase in the probability of observing a "Nay" vote. However, for a district at the 75 percentile, with a relatively economically important manufacturing base, a similar change in land concentration suggests only a 0.12 increase in the probability of a "No".[11]

---

[11] Clearly, we cannot rule out the possibility that the extent of manufacturing share (or of national bank share, see below) was endogenous – areas where agrarian interests were stronger held back financial development and hence industrialization. This is not inconsistent with our point that the extent of

National banks obviously stood to gain from the Act's passage, possibly at the expense of small state unit banks, and we next explore the association between the existing structure of the local banking system and local political support for the act. In Table 4 Column 2, we include the share of national banks in total banks within the district in 1920 (and thus unaffected by the Act's passage in 1927). The coefficient estimate indicates that congressional opposition to the Act was significantly attenuated in those districts in which national banks were more dominant in the local banking system. A one standard deviation increase in this share suggests a 0.05 decline in the probability of observing a "Nay" vote.

Clearly, districts with few banks or with smaller banks may have been differentially disposed to vote on the legislation. To proxy for the relative number of such banks, we include the per capita number of state banks, and to proxy for bank size, we include the average value of deposits in each state bank in the district in Table 4B Column 3. Of course, these "explanatory" variables are endogenous since we have argued that bank structure is shaped by landed interests, and we must be careful in drawing strong conclusions from this exercise. Nevertheless, it is interesting that in Table 4B Column 3, the coefficient on land concentration remains significant, and increases in magnitude.

The debate over the McFadden Act occurred against a backdrop of banking sector distress in the country side, as many small state banks failed during the 1920s bust in commodity prices. This distress could perhaps have shaped preferences over regulations, and also affected the relative power of the various interest groups in the battle over the

industrialization is a proxy for the political power of agrarian interests, which is all we want to draw from this exercise.

act. In Column 4, we include the state bank suspension rate over the period 1921-25 to help proxy for financial sector distress within the congressional district. The coefficient for land concentration remains significantly positive, while the bank suspension rate is negative and not significant.[12]

Pre-existing state level branching regulations may also illustrate the impact of local constituencies on congressional support. Specifically, while the McFadden Act was in part focused on equalizing the regulatory environment surrounding branching between national and state banks, it was viewed by its opponents more generally as a fundamental step towards more widespread bank branching. Thus, opposition to the McFadden Act among local constituencies would have been expected to even be more vigorous in those states that did not already permit branching, fearing that the Act's passage would embolden supporters of branching.[13]

We explore this hypothesis in columns 5 and 6 of Table 4B, estimating separately the baseline specification for the subsample of districts located in states that did allow bank branching in 1920 (column 5), and those that did not allow branching (column 6). Among the unit banking states, the impact of land concentration on the probability of observing a "Nay" vote is about two thirds higher than the overall sample in column 2 of

---

[12] That we do not find these district level factors to matter does not mean they have no influence on a congressman's attitude. To the extent that a state adopts a common position, say because of widespread state-level distress, it will be reflected in the state vote. Our test is calibrated to pick up the incremental constituency position.

[13] State regulators themselves may have had an interest in the act, as the possible expansion of national banks and branching may have affected regulatory rents. There is for example some evidence that features of the state regulatory system may have been designed for rent seeking at the expense of stability in the 1930s (Mitchener (2007)). However, we find no evidence that measures of the state regulatory system, from data kindly provided by Kris Mitchener, such as the length of the supervisor's term and whether the supervisor had the power to charter or liquidate banks, shaped congressional opposition to the act—these results are available upon request.

Table 4A, suggesting that in those states already opposed to branching and concerned about its spread, the influence of local land interests on the vote appeared to have been substantial. In contrast, the land concentration coefficient in the subsample of states allowing branching is considerably smaller, and not significant.

Several states shifted to branching in the 1920s, while a few passed more restrictive branching laws during the decade (Dehejia and Lleras-Muney (2008)). However, the observed differences in estimates are qualitatively similar if we use branching regulations observed in 1930 (columns 7 and 8).

This larger positive association between land concentration and the likelihood of voting against the Act in non-branching states suggests that perhaps the incentives of landed interests to oppose the Act may have been especially strong in those states that did not have branching in the 1920s. Equally, the forces for branch banking (and hence for McFadden) may have been inherently weaker in these states, which is why they did not have branch banking in the first place. Indeed, Rajan and Ramcharan (2011) find that states with more concentrated landholdings were less likely to have bank branching. It is not possible for us to tell apart the greater desire and incentive in unit banking states to oppose the act from the possibility that anti-branching advocates were more influential in those states.

Cost and Availability of Credit

Our hypothesis is that the opposition to the McFadden Act was largely driven by the desire of incumbents to preserve the local market structure in order to protect rents. We now investigate this hypothesis more directly. We collected by hand several county level indicators of local land mortgage loans from the 1930 US Census archives. We have

24

the average interest on farm mortgages held by banks, a proxy for the cost of credit. We also have data on the fraction of indebted farms, and the debt to value ratio for farms. Finally, we have the amount of bank mortgage credit, which when scaled by local state bank deposits, gives us a credit to deposit ratio, a standard measure of local credit activity.

Of course, it is possible to argue against each of these variables taken alone as a measure of local rents – they could be a measure of effective demand, as determined both by the need for credit as well as the creditworthiness of the borrower. However, assuming the underlying distribution of creditworthiness after correcting for economic, geographic, and demographic variables is the largely similar across counties, the simultaneous prevalence of lower interest rates and higher credit volumes is more consistent with higher supply and less rents. The simple correlations in Table 5 suggest that counties with lower interest rates also had a greater fraction of indebted farms and higher loan to value ratios. To focus further on common supply side factors, we extract the principal component from our four proxies for access to credit. The first component explains about 41% of the variance in the data, nearly twice as much as the second component. Moreover, it correlates negatively with interest rates and positively with the proxies for credit volume; the share of indebted farms, the debt to value ratio, and the mortgage credit to deposit ratio, suggesting that the first component might be a useful summary measure of local credit supply conditions.

In Table 6A, we examine the impact of these credit variables on voting outcomes. There is evidence that congressmen in districts with higher interest rates and less credit availability were more likely to vote against the Act. In Table 6A Column 1, for example, a one standard deviation increase in the interest rate is associated with a 0.21 increase in the probability of a "Nay" vote. However, the statistical significance of these estimates is generally weak. We should note that since these credit variables are observed about three years after Act's passage, they could reflect the impact of the Act rather than simple rent preservation.

To address this issue, we instrument the 1930 district level credit variables with 1920 land concentration. Land concentration in 1920 is observed well before the Act's introduction in Congress, and it can be taken as predetermined. There is also substantial evidence that landed interests restrained the number of banks in order to restrict credit and make it more expensive at the county level (see Rajan and Ramcharan (2011)). When conditioned on a wide array of district level observables, the 1920 land concentration variable is also likely to satisfy the exclusion restriction assumption.

In Table 6B, the IV estimates using land concentration as an instrument are uniformly significant and economically large. A one standard deviation increase in the fraction of indebted farms within the district (signifying greater availability of credit) is associated with a decline in the probability of observing congressional opposition to the Act by 0.2. A similar increase in state bank lending, scaled by deposits, suggests a 0.46 drop in the probability of a "Nay" vote, suggesting that congressional opposition to the Act was significantly more likely in districts with less credit availability. The coefficient on the principal component—the summary measure of district credit supply conditions— is also negative and statistically significant.

To gauge the robustness of this identification strategy, in column 6 we use average rainfall as an instrument. The coefficient estimate for the principal component is nearly identical to column 5, though less precisely estimated. The noisier estimates may, as we have argued, result from the noise introduced by aggregating rainfall across a district.

In sum, districts where credit was less easily available, and more costly when available, tended to vote against the act, even though its primary intent was to level the playing field and increase bank competition.

B. Final House Roll Call, Jan 1927

The House bill that was initially passed contained the Hull amendments which "…limit branch banking to those States which permitted branch banking at the time of the approval of the bill – so far as the national banking and the Federal Reserve System are concerned." This was an attempt to defang the opposition of the congressmen from unit-banking states, who were worried that national banks and state bank members of the Federal Reserve System might join hands after the passage of the Act to push for branch banking in their states. By limiting the branching powers of national banks to only those states that allowed branch banking at the time of the Act, national banks elsewhere would continue to have an incentive to oppose branch banking.

The Senate Committee eliminated both the Hull amendments as well as some limitations on post-Act branching imposed on state members of the Federal Reserve System. In May 1926, the Senate passed the bill in its Senate Committee form. The differences between the House and the Senate were finally overcome when the House adopted a resolution on Jan 24th 1927, accepting all the important amendments to the bill made by the Senate Committee. Bitter recriminations followed.

It was alleged that advocates of the bill in the House had made a deal with supporters of farm-relief legislation. Specifically, it was alleged that the McNary-Haugen Farm Bill, which originally included government price support for grain, was extended to cotton and tobacco allegedly in order to entice the Southern delegation to support the McFadden Bill. Price supports for plantation crops would have greatly benefitted landed interests, especially those in plantation districts. We now investigate the role of landed interests in explaining the switch in the House position on the Hull Amendment, which led to the Act's passage.

In Table 7 column 1, the dependent variable is 1 if the representative voted against the final vote in favor of the Senate's position on the bill (Jan 24th). At first glance, there is little significant relationship between the vote and land concentration in the district and in fact, the coefficient estimate is negative. But, we now focus on the switching decision. To this end, we create an indicator variable that equals 1 if a House member switched his vote from opposing the compromise proposition in place of the Hull Amendment on June 24, 1926 (which was agreed in the Senate-House conference committee in an attempt to reconcile the two versions of the bill) to finally accepting the Senate compromise on January 24, 1927. The indicator variable equals 0 if there was no change in the member's position across the two votes. In column 2, there is a robust positive association between the probability of vote switching and land concentration.

Of course, the concentration of agrarian land holdings is most often associated with plantation crops such as tobacco. And to examine whether the inclusion of such crops in the McNary-Haugen Farm Bill led to the change in support for the McFadden Act, we turn to the 1910 Agricultural Census, which records detailed county level data on crop values, including the value of tobacco grown—cotton values are not available. We aggregate these data up to the congressional district level, and create the share of tobacco in the value of total crops grown in the district. We interact this variable with land concentration, and include it both linearly and through a squared term to control for any direct impact it might have on explaining the switch. Finally, we present separate estimates for states that allowed branching and those that did not.

The results are striking. Among the non branching states (Table 7 Column 3), where opposition to the Senate's weakening of the Hull Amendment was most concentrated, the interaction term between land concentration and the value of tobacco grown in the district from the 1910 census is positive and significant; the individual linear terms are also significant at the one percent level. For a district at the median level of tobacco intensity, a one standard deviation increase in land concentration is associated with a 0.22 increase in the probability that the Congressman switched his vote. However, for a district dominated by tobacco—one at the 90 percent level of tobacco intensity—a similar increase in land concentration suggests a 0.28 increase in the probability of observing a switch from a "Nay" on the June 26, 1926 compromise intended to reconcile the Senate and House versions of the act, to a "Yea" in January 1927, ensuring final passage.

For the branching states, where the Hull amendment would have played little part, there is no evidence that tobacco played a significant role in explaining the limited switching observed in those districts (Table 7 Column 4), though the coefficient estimates have their expected signs.[14]

---

[14] We also replicate this switching analysis for the final 1927 vote with respect to the February 4th 1926 vote. The results are qualitatively similar.

Taken together, the evidence suggests that in order to protect their rents, landed interests opposed the McFadden Act, and were able to influence the congressional vote, especially in those districts in which they held greater economic clout. But in exchange for the possibility of lucrative price supports for key crops, landed interest were in the end willing to acquiesce on bank competition. We next examine the impact of the Act's passage on the local bank structure.

IV. RESULTS: IMPACT OF MCFADDEN ACT ON LOCAL BANK STRUCTURES

The previous section has showed that landed interests were pivotal constituencies in influencing the vote on the McFadden Act. Were the fears of enhanced competition correct? Among those states that already had branching, did the Act's passage redress the disadvantage that national banks had vis a vis state banks?

To address this question, we turn to county level data on banks over the period 1921-1930. In Table 8 Column 1, we use the log change in the average number of national banks over the period 1927-1930, relative to 1926—the year before the Act's passage as the dependent variable. We exclude the post 1930 period, which was highly unstable. The branching indicator variable equals 1 for those counties located in states permitting branching before the Act's passage, and 0 otherwise. The estimate in Table 8 Column 1 suggests that after the Act's passage, the number of national banks was about 3.1 percentage points higher relative to 1926 in those counties located in branching states. Column 2 includes our standard county-level demographic and geographic controls, and here the estimated impact of the Act is larger and more precisely estimated at 4.4 percentage points.

To discern whether the apparent impact of the Act on national banks might have been part of a broader trend, affecting state banks as well, we include the change in the share of national banks within the county as the dependent variable in Table 8 Column 3. The coefficient estimate suggests the share of national banks increased after the Act's passage in counties located in states that had bank branching, suggesting that the Act disproportionately affected national banks in those branching counties.

Does the increase in national bank shares after the Act's passage stem from new national bank entrants rather than the failure of state banks? To check this, the dependent variable in Table 8 column 4 is the failure rate of state banks, defined as the ratio of state bank failures to the number of state banks the previous year, and averaged over the 1927-1930 period. After controlling for county level characteristics, including the state bank failure rate in 1926, there is no evidence that the state bank failure rate was higher in counties permitting branching during the 1927-1930 period. This suggests that new national bank entry, rather than disproportionate state bank failure, was responsible for the increase in national bank share.

V. Conclusion

This paper has examined the role of constituencies in shaping the development of the financial system, using evidence from congressional voting on the McFadden Act of 1927. This act regulated the relationship between state and national banks in the United States for decades, and at the time, it was viewed as a precursor to more widespread bank branching, engendering opposition from rural interests and incumbent banks concerned about greater competition and a diminution of rents.

We find evidence that House representatives from districts with more concentrated land holdings (our proxy for the relative importance of landed interests) were far more likely to oppose the McFadden Act during its first House vote in January 1926. The association of land concentration with congressional opposition was especially strong in those districts where agriculture was relatively more important than manufacturing, suggesting that landed elites were politically more effective when they also dominated economically. Measures of the size of incumbent rents, such as the interest rate, also positively predicted congressional opposition. And consistent with historical narratives suggesting that political horse trading eventually led to the act's passage, there is evidence that landed interests supported the act in exchange for key agricultural price supports – interestingly temporary relief measures bought support that had long term effects through legislation. Finally, examining the immediate impact of the act, we find evidence of greater national bank entry in those states that permitted branching.

These results suggest that the constituencies or interest groups that arise from the technology of economic production can shape important economic institutions by using existing political institutions and the legislative process rather than through coercive control of the state and the threat of force (Stigler (1971)). In addition, long after landed interests ceased to be a political force, the McFadden Act endured for many decades, as new politically influential interest groups, like small community banks, emerged in the wake of the act and sought to maintain the status quo. Thus, constituencies can have an influence on economic outcomes long after the initial actors have passed from the scene.

TABLES AND FIGURES

Table 1: Variables' Definitions and Sources

Variable	Source	Definition
Land Inequality (Gini Coefficient)	United States Bureau of Census; Inter-University Consortium for Political and Social Research (ICPSR) NOs: 0003, 0007,0008,0009,0014,0017	The number of farms are distributed across the following size (acres) bins: 3-9; 10-19 acres; 20-49 acres; 50-99 acres; 100-174;175-259;260-499;500-999; 1000 and above. We use the mid point of each bin to construct the Gini coefficient; farms above 1000 acres are assumed to be 1000 acres. The Gini coefficient is given by $$1+1/n-\left[2/(m*n^2)\right]\sum_{i=1}^{n}\left(n-i+1\right)y_i$$ Where farms are ranked in ascending order of size, y_i, and n is the total number of farms, while m is the mean farm size. [Atkinson, A.B. (1970)]. At the state level, we sum the total number of farms in each bin across counties, then compute the Gini coefficient.
Number of State and National Banks Active in each county.	Federal Deposit Insurance Corporation Data on Banks in the United States, 1920-1936 (ICPSR 07).	
Urban Population; Fraction of Black Population; Fraction of Population Between 7 and 20 years; County Area; County Population; Value of Crops/ Farm Land Divided by Farm Population	United States Bureau of Census; Inter-University Consortium for Political and Social Research (ICPSR) NOs: 0003, 0007,0008,0009,0014,0017	
Distance From Mississippi River; Atlantic; Pacific and the Great Lakes.	Computed Using ArcView from each county's centroid.	
Voting Roll Call Data, on McFadden Act., Ideology of Legislator	www.voteview.com	
Rainfall (Mean and Standard Deviation)	Weather Source 10 Woodsom Drive Amesbury MA, 0193 (Data Compiled from the National Weather Service Cooperative (COOP) Network	The COOP Network consists of more than 20,000 sites across the U.S. and has monthly precipitation observations for the past 100 years. However, for a station's data to be included in the county level data, the station needs to have a minimum of 10 years history and minimum data density of 90 percent: ratio of number of actual observations to potential observations. If one or more candidate stations meet the above criteria the stations' data are averaged to produce the county level observations—which we then aggregate further up to the congressional district. The arithmetic mean and standard deviation of rainfall are computed from the monthly data for all years with available data.

Figure 1. Land Inequality, Box Plots, by Region, 1920

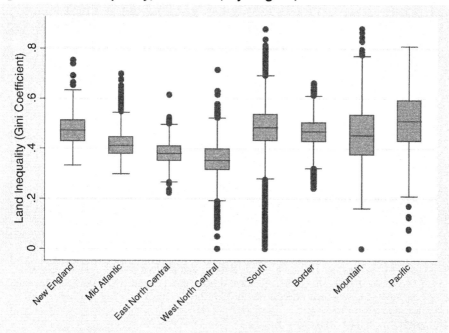

The shaded rectangle represents the interquartile range of the Gini coefficient across districts in the region. The range contains the median—the solid line. The ends of the vertical lines extend to a maximum of 1.5 times the interquartile range. Dots beyond this range are possible outliers.

Table 2: Pairwise Correlations

	Land Concentration	Basic cereals	Grains and Seeds	Hay and forage	Fruits and Nuts	Vegetables	Avg Annual rainfall	Standard deviation of rainfall	Avg temperature
Land Concentration	1								
Basic cereals	-0.446**	1							
Grains and Seeds	-0.048*	-0.024	1						
Hay and forage	-0.175*	-0.159**	-0.023	1					
Fruits and Nuts	0.341**	-0.284**	-0.049**	-0.016	1				
Vegetables	0.299**	-0.377**	-0.028**	0.063*	0.163**	1			
Average Annual rainfall	0.346**	-0.212**	-0.167**	-0.461**	0.042**	0.118**	1		
Standard deviation of rainfall	0.360**	-0.171*	-0.059**	0.332**	0.148**	0.135**	0.661**	1	
Average temperature	0.436**	-0.223*	-0.009	0.617**	0.082**	-0.065**	0.498**	0.532**	1

This table presents the pairwise correlations between land concentration, crop shares, and measures of rainfall in the districts. Crop shares are shares of land devoted to the crop within the county as measured in the 1920 census. Rainfall is measured over the period 1900-2000.
* denotes significance at the 10% level
** denotes significance at the 5% level or higher.

Table 3A. McFadden Act Roll Call, February 1926.

Vote	Full Sample			Available Sample	
	Number	Percent		Number	Percent
Yea	289	67		233	66
Paired Yea	4	0.9		4	1
Paired Nay	3	0.7		2	0.6
Nay	91	21		84	23
Present	8	2		8	2
Not Voting	32	7		23	6
Total	427			354	

Table 3B. McFadden Act Roll Call, February 1926, By Region

	New England		Mid Atlantic		East North Central		West North Central	
	Number	Percent	Number	Percent	Number	Percent	Number	Percent
Yea	19	86	41	76	62	82	33	62
Paired Yea	1	5	2	4	1	1		
Paired Nay					1	1		
Nay			1		10	13	15	28
Present			3	6			1	2
Not Voting	2	2	7	13	2	3	4	8
Total	22		54		76		53	

	South		Border		Mountain		Pacific	
	Number	Percent	Number	Percent	Number	Percent	Number	Percent
Yea	42	46	17	67	8	80	11	69
Paired Yea	1	1	9	29				
Paired Nay								
Nay	46	50			2	20	1	6
Present	2	2	1	3			1	6
Not Voting	1	1	4	13			3	19
Total	92		31		10		16	

A "Pair" occurs when the leaders of the two parties both have members who want to be absent from the vote. If one member would vote "Yea" and the opposite "Nay" then the leadership would "pair" them so that their absence would not affect the outcome of the roll call.

Figure 2. Land Concentration and McFadden Act (1926) Congressional Votes

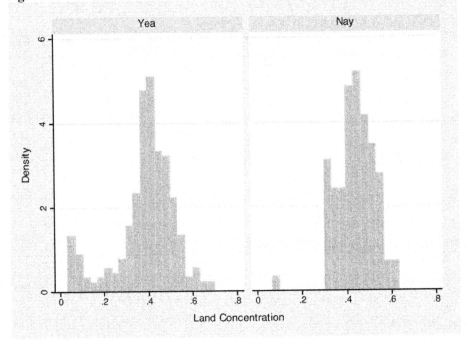

Table 4A. The McFadden Act, The Initial Bill, February 1926.
Dependent Variable: Nay (1), Voted Yea (0).

VARIABLES	(1) *No Controls*	(2) *Geographic, Demographic and Ideology Controls*	(3) *Per Capita Farm Wealth*	(4) *IV*	(5) *2SLS*
Land Concentration (Log)	0.246**	0.534**	0.552**	0.974*	1.058**
	(0.109)	(0.227)	(0.247)	(0.583)	(0.501)
Per Capita Farm Wealth			0.0735		
			(0.448)		
Observations	317	317	317	317	317
R-squared	0.503	0.534	0.543	0.59	

Standard errors clustered at the state level. *** $p<0.01$, ** $p<0.05$, * $p<0.1$. All regressions include state level indicators. Columns 2-5 also include the distance from the Mississippi River; the Atlantic Ocean; the Great Lakes; the Pacific Ocean (all distances in log kilometers); the black population; the illiterate population; the number of 5-17 year olds; the urban population (all expressed as a share of total district population); the district area (in log square miles) and population (log) are also included; and the two DW nominate scores for the legislator in each district (preference for redistribution and the urban-rural bias (Poole and Rosenthal (2007)). In column 4, land concentration is instrumented using average rainfall in the district. The first stage coefficient estimate for average rainfall is 0.17 and the t-statistic is 4.03. In column 5, we use both average rainfall and its standard deviation in the instrument set. The first stage coefficient estimates are 0.09 (p-value 0.04) and 0.12 (p-value=0.01) respectively. The F-Statistic for joint significance is 9.82 (p-value=0.00). The Hansen J-Statistic (for the over-identification test) is 0.13 (p-value=0.72).

Table 4B. The McFadden Act, The Initial Bill, February 1926.
Dependent Variable: Nay (1), Voted Yea (0).

VARIABLES	(1) Manufacturing	(2) National Banks	(3) State Banks	(4) State Bank Failures	(5) Branching States 1920	(6) Non Branching States 1920	(7) Branching States 1930	(8) Non Branching States 1930
Land Concentration (Log)	1.018**	0.532**	0.683***	0.671***	0.139	0.709***	0.129	0.575**
	(0.380)	(0.217)	(0.241)	(0.244)	(0.473)	(0.266)	(0.416)	(0.275)
Land Concentration (Log)* Manufacturing	-0.733*							
	(0.443)							
Manufacturing	-1.887**							
	(0.795)							
Manufacturing, squared	1.145**							
	(0.548)							
Share of National Banks, 1920		-0.270*						
		(0.160)						
State Banks Per Capita, 1920			416.6**	407.3*				
			(204.8)	(205.2)				
Ratio of State Bank Deposits to Number of State Banks, 1920			-1.630	-1.430				
			(2.980)	2.99				
State bank suspensions rate, 1921-1925				-1.043				
				(1.671)				
Observations	314	317	317	317	92	225	157	160
R-squared	0.562	0.538	0.542	0.543	0.272	0.63	0.41	0.74

Standard errors clustered at the state level. *** p<0.01, ** p<0.05, * p<0.1. All regressions include state level indicators. All columns include the distance from the Mississippi River; the Atlantic Ocean; the Great Lakes; the Pacific Ocean (all distances in log kilometers); the black population; the illiterate population; the number of 5-17 year olds; the urban population (all expressed as a share of total district population); the district area (in log square miles) and population (log) are also included; and the two DW nominate scores for the legislator in each district (preference for redistribution and the urban-rural bias (Poole and Rosenthal (2007)). The state bank suspension rate is the number of state banks suspended from 1921-1925 divided by the number of state banks in 1920.

Table 5. Simple County Level Correlations, Credit Variables

	Mortgage Interest Rate	Mortgage Debt to Farm Values	Fraction of Indebted Farms	Ratio of Mortgage Debt to Banks Deposits	Principal Component
Mortgage Interest Rate	1				
Mortgage Debt to Farm Values	-0.1845*	1			
Fraction of Indebted Farms	-0.3365*	0.2977*	1		
Ratio of Mortgage Debt to State Bank Deposits	0.0029	0.2473*	0.0975*	1	
Principal Component	-0.6366*	0.7130*	0.7663*	0.3844*	1

Table 6A. The McFadden Act, The Initial Bill, 1926 & The Cost & Availability of Credit.

Dependent Variable: Nay (1), Voted Yea (0). OLS Estimates

	(1)	(2)	(3)	(4)	(5)
Interest Rate	0.201* (0.114)				
Fraction of Indebted Farms		-0.339 (0.323)			
Mortgage Debt, as a Share of State Bank			0.00504 (0.0254)		
Mortgage Debt as a Share of Farm Value				0.00154 (0.00480)	
Principal Component					-0.0360 (0.0394)
Observations	316	316	316	316	316
R-squared	0.531	0.542	0.536	0.531	0.534

Table 6B. IV Estimates

	(1)	(2)	(3)	(4)	(5)	(6)
Interest Rate	1.057* (0.566)					
Fraction of Indebted Farms		-2.215** (0.900)				
Mortgage Debt, as a Share of State Bank			-0.635* (0.341)			
Mortgage Debt as a Share of Farm Value				-0.0262** (0.0109)		
Principal Component					-0.173*** (0.0648)	-0.166 (0.125)
Observations	316	316	316	316	316	316
R-squared	0.531	0.542	0.536	0.531	0.516	0.58
First Stage						
Land Concentration	0.503	-0.239	-20.24	-0.832	-3.054	
F-Statistic	3.880	22.69	45.38	1.98	86.78	
(p-value)	(0.06)	(0.00)	(0.00)	0.167	(0.00)	

Standard errors clustered at the state level. *** $p<0.01$, ** $p<0.05$, * $p<0.1$. All regressions include state level indicators. All columns include the distance from the Mississippi River; the Atlantic Ocean; the Great Lakes; the Pacific Ocean (all distances in log kilometers); the black population; the illiterate population; the number of 5-17 year olds; the urban population (all expressed as a share of total district population); the district area (in log square miles) and population (log) are also included; and the two DW nominate scores for the legislator in each district (preference for redistribution and the urban-rural bias (Poole and Rosenthal (2007)). Column 6 instruments the principal component with average rainfall. The first stage coefficient for average rainfall (log) is -0.93 (p-value=0.04).

Table 7. The McFadden Act, The Final Bill, 1927

	(1)	(2)	(3)	(4)
	1927 Roll Call Vote Nay (1), Voted Yea (0)	Vote Switching Yes (1) No(0)	Vote Switching Yes (1) No(0)	Vote Switching Yes (1) No(0)
			Non Branching States	Branching States
		Hull Amendment (June 26, 1926)		
Land Concentration	-0.356	0.716**	1.068***	-0.231
	(0.262)	(0.311)	(0.388)	(1.445)
Land Concentration (Log)* Tobacco Value Share			9.394**	2.732
			(4.095)	(8.573)
Tobacco Value Share			7.637**	2.117
			(3.353)	(9.796)
Tobacco Value Share, Squared			4.029	0.033
			(4.249)	(19.36)
Observations	294	228	153	56
R-squared	0.583	0.511	0.567	0.546

Standard errors clustered at the state level. *** p<0.01, ** p<0.05, * p<0.1. All regressions include state level indicators. Columns 1-4 also include the distance from the Mississippi River; the Atlantic Ocean; the Great Lakes; the Pacific Ocean (all distances in log kilometers); the black population; the illiterate population; the number of 5-17 year olds; the urban population (all expressed as a share of total district population); the district area (in log square miles) and population (log) are also included; and the two DW nominate scores for the legislator in each district (preference for redistribution and the urban-rural bias (Poole and Rosenthal (2007)). The dependent variable in columns 2-4 equal 1 if a congressional district switched from a "Nay" in the 1926 Hull Amendment vote to a "Yea" vote in 1927 and 0 if the vote remained the same.

Table 8. The Impact of the McFadden Act in a County Level Cross Section.

VARIABLES	(1) Change in Number of National Banks	(2) Change in Number of National Banks	(3) Change in Share of National Banks	(4) State Bank Failure Rate, 1927-1930
Branching	3.125*	4.408**	4.042**	-0.226
	(1.768)	(1.712)	(1.779)	(0.819)
Observations	2163	2082	2108	2761
R-squared	0.011	0.031	0.020	0.044

The dependent variable in columns (1) and (2) is the difference between the log of the average number of national banks in county i from 1927-1930 and the log number of national banks in 1926 in county i. Branching is an indicator variable that equals 1 if a state allowed branching, and 0 otherwise, observed in 1920. Column 1 also includes the log number of banks in 1926 in county i as a control variable. Column 2 also includes additional controls include the distance from the Mississippi River; the Atlantic Ocean; the Great Lakes; the Pacific Ocean (all distances in log kilometers); the black population; the illiterate population; the number of 5-17 year olds; the urban population (all expressed as a share of total district population); the district area (in log square miles) and population (log) are also included; and the two DW nominate scores for the legislator in each district (preference for redistribution and the urban-rural bias (Poole and Rosenthal (2007)).The dependent variable in column 3 is the difference in the average share of national banks in county i computed over the period 1927-1930 relative to the share in 1926. Controls include the share of national banks in 1926, as well as the previous geographic and demographic controls in column 2. In column 4, the dependent variable is the average of the annual state bank suspension rate over the period 1927-1930. The annual state bank suspension rate itself is computed as the ratio of the number suspended state banks in the calendar year relative to the total number of state banks the previous year. The controls in column 4 include the state bank suspension rate in 1926, as well as the previous demographic and geographic controls. Standard errors are clustered at the state level. ***, **, * denote significance at the 1, 5 and 10 percent respectively.

References

Acemoglu, Daron, Simon Johnson, and James A. Robinson, 2005, Institutions as fundamental determinants of long-run growth, in Philippe Aghion and Steven N. Durlauf, eds.: *Handbook of Economic Growth* Volume 1A (North-Holland Publishing, Amsterdam).

Acharya, Viral, Stijn van Nieuwerburgh, Matthew Richardson and Larry White, *Guaranteed to Fail: Fannie Mae, Freddie Mac and the Debacle of Mortgage Finance*, c) Princeton University Press, March 2011

Adler, Edward. Why Congressional Reforms Fail: Reelection and the House Committee System. Chicago: University of Chicago Press, 2002.

Alston, Lee and Joseph Ferrie. Paternalism in agricultural labor contracts in the US South: Implications for the growth of the welfare state. American Economic Review (1993) vol. 83 (4) pp. 852-876

Alston, Lee and Kauffman, Kyle. Agricultural Chutes and Ladders: New Estimates of Sharecroppers and "True Tenants" in the South, 1900–1920. The Journal of Economic History (2009) vol. 57 (02) pp. 464-475

American Bankers Association. (1935). The Bank Chartering History and Policies of the United States. Monograph. Economic Policy Commission.

Brown, Craig, and Serdar Dinc, "The Politics of Bank Failures: Evidence from Emerging Markets", Quarterly Journal of Economics, 2005 (November), 120 (4), 1413-1444.

Calomiris, Charles, and Carlos Ramirez, 2004, The political economy of bank entry restrictions: theory and evidence from the US in the 1920s, Columbia University Working Paper.

Cartinhour, Gaines Thomson, and Ray Bert Westerfield, 1980, *Branch, Group, and Chain Banking. Arno Press: New York,*

Cetorelli, Nicola and Philip Strahan, "Finance As A Barrier To Entry: Bank Competition And Industry Structure In U.S. Local Markets", 2006, *Journal of Finance* 61(1), 437-61.

Chapman, John, 1934, *Concentration of Banking: The Changing Structure and Control of Banking in the United States* (Columbia University Press, New York, NY).

Collins, Charles Wallace. 1926. "The Branch Banking Question," MacMillian, New York.

Do, Quy-Toan, 2004, "Institutional Trap", World Bank working paper.

Dehejia, Rajiv and Adriana Lleras-Muney. 2007. "Financial Development and Pathways of Growth: State Branching and Deposit Insurance Laws in the United States from 1900 to 1940", *Journal of Law and Economics,* Vol. 50, May.

Dinc, Serdar, "Politicians and Banks: Political Influences on Government-Owned Banks in Emerging Markets", 2005 (August), Journal of Financial Economics, 77, 453-479.

Economides, Nicholas, with R. Glenn Hubbard and Darius Palia. The Political Economy of Branching Restrictions and Deposit Insurance: A Model of Monopolistic Competition of Small and Large Banks, *Journal of Law and Economics* vol. XXXIX (October 1996), pp. 667-704.

Engerman, Stanley, and Kenneth Sokoloff, 2002, Factor endowments, inequality, and paths of development among new world economies, *Economía* 3, 1, 41-109.

Engerman, Stanley and Kenneth Sokoloff, 2003, Institutional and non-institutional explanations of economic differences, NBER Working Paper 9989.

Fishback, Price. (1989), "Debt Peonage in Postbellum Georgia." *Explorations in Economic History*
26, 219–236.

Galor, Oded, Omer Moav and Dietrich Vollrath. 2009. "Inequality in Land ownership, the Emergence of Human Capital Promoting Institutions and the Great Divergence" (*Review of Economic Studies*, 76, 143-179

Glaeser, Edward, Jose Scheinkman, and Andrei Shleifer, 2003, *The* Injustice of Inequality, *Journal of Monetary Economics*, Elsevier, vol. 50(1), pages 199-222, January.

Goodwyn, Lawrence, 1978, *The Populist Moment: A Short History of the Agrarian Revolt in America* (Oxford University Press, New York, NY).

Haber, Stephen, 2005, Political institutions and financial development: evidence from the economic histories of Mexico and the United States, unpublished manuscript.

Haney, L., 1914, Farm credit conditions in a cotton state, *The American Economic Review*, 14, 1, 47-67.

Hicks, John D., 1931, *Populist Revolt: A History of the Farmers' Alliance and the People's Party* (University of Minnesota Press, Minneapolis, MN).

Igan, Deniz, Prachi Mishra, and Thierry Tressel, "A Fistful of Dollars: Lobbying and the Financial Crisis", IMF Working Paper, 2011.

Klebaner, Benjamin J. (1990) *American Commercial Banking: A History* Boston: Twayne Publishers.

Kroszner, Randall S. and Philip E. Strahan "What Drives Deregulation? Economics and Politics of the Relaxation of Bank Branching Restrictions."; *Quarterly Journal of Economics*, 1999, *114*(4), pp. 1437-67.

Mian, Atif, Amir Sufi and Francesco Trebbi; "The Political Economy of the US Mortgage Default Crisis." American Economic Review, 2010, 100(5), pp. 1967-98.

Mitchener, Kris James. "Are Supervision and Regulation Pillars of Financial Stability? Evidence from the Great Depression," *Journal of Law and Economics* 50 (May 2007), 273-302,

Pred, A., 1966, *The Spatial Implication of U.S. Industrial Growth* (MIT Press, Cambridge, MA).

Preston, H. "The McFadden Banking Act," American Economic Review (1927) vol. 17 (2) pp. 201-218.

Poole, Keith T. and Howard Rosenthal. 2007. Ideology and Congress. Piscataway, N.J.: Transaction Press.

Rajan, Raghuram and Rodney Ramcharan, 2010, Land and Credit: A Study of the Political Economy of Banking in the United States in the Early 20th Century, forthcoming, *Journal of Finance.*

Ransom, Roger, and Richard Sutch, 2001, *One Kind of Freedom: The Economic Consequences of Emancipation* (Cambridge University Press, Cambridge, U.K.).

Rusk, Jerrold G. 2001. A Statistical History of the American Electorate. CQ Press: Washington DC.

Report of the Comptroller of Currency. 1922. U.S. Federal Reserve Board.

Southworth, Donald Shirley. 1928. Branch Banking in the United States. McGraw-Hill: New York.

White, Eugene, "Voting for Costly Regulation: Evidence from Banking Referenda in Illinois, 1924", *Southern Economic Journal*, Vol. 51, No. 4 (Apr., 1985), pp. 1084-1098

CPSIA information can be obtained at www.ICGtesting.com
Printed in the USA
BVOW09s1143100516

447494BV00017B/232/P